Pebble® Plus

Hands-On Science Fun

# How to Build a TORNADO in a BOTTLE

Revised Edition

by Lori Shores

**Consultant:** Ronald Browne, PhD
Department of Elementary & Early Childhood Education
Minnesota State University, Mankato

CAPSTONE PRESS
a capstone imprint

This is a Capstone 4D book!

Want fun videos that go with this book?

Just visit www.capstone4d.com

Use this password

**tornado.09441**

Pebble Plus is published by Capstone Press,
1710 Roe Crest Drive, North Mankato, Minnesota 56003
www.capstonepub.com

Copyright © 2018 by Capstone Press, a Capstone imprint.
All rights reserved. No part of this publication may be reproduced in whole or in part, or stored in a retrieval system, or transmitted in any form or by any means, electronic, mechanical, photocopying, recording, or otherwise, without written permission of the publisher.

**Library of Congress Cataloging-in-Publication Data**
Names: Shores, Lori, author.
Title: How to build a tornado in a bottle / by Lori Shores.
Description: [2018 edition]. | North Mankato, Minnesota: Capstone Press, [2018] | Series: Hands-on science fun | Series: A 4D book | Audience: Age 4–8.
Identifiers: LCCN 2017044222 (print)
LCCN 2017048004 (ebook)
ISBN 9781543509564 (eBook PDF)
ISBN 9781543509441 (hardcover)
ISBN 9781543509502 (paperback)
Subjects: LCSH: Tornadoes—Juvenile literature. | Science—Experiments—Juvenile literature.
Classification: LCC QC955.2 (ebook) | LCC QC955.2 .S54 2018 (print) | DDC 551.55/3078—dc23
LC record available at https://lccn.loc.gov/2017044222

**Editorial Credits**
Marissa Kirkman, editor; Sarah Bennett, designer; Tracy Cummins, media researcher; Tori Abraham, production specialist

**Photo Credits**
Capstone Studio: Karon Dubke, Cover, 3, 5, 6, 7, 9, 11, 13, 15, 19, 21; Dreamstime: Chris White, 17; Shutterstock: ArtMari, Design Element Cover and Interior, Rafai Fabrykiewicz, 4-5 Background

## Note to Parents and Teachers

The Hands-On Science Fun set supports national science standards related to physical science. This book describes and illustrates building a tornado in a bottle. The images support early readers in understanding the text. The repetition of words and phrases helps early readers learn new words. This book also introduces early readers to subject-specific vocabulary words, which are defined in the Glossary section. Early readers may need assistance to read some words and to use the Table of Contents, Glossary, Read More, Internet Sites, Critical Thinking Questions, and Index sections of the book.

Printed in the United States 5488

# Table of Contents


Getting Started . . . . . 4

Making a Tornado in a Bottle . . . . . 6

How Does It Work?. . . . . 16

Glossary . . . . . 22

Read More. . . . . 23

Internet Sites . . . . . 23

Critical Thinking Questions . . . . . 24

Index . . . . . 24


**Safety Note:**
Please ask an adult for help in building your tornado in a bottle.

# Getting Started

The rain pours
and the wind roars.
Tornadoes can be scary.
But there's nothing scary
about a tornado in a bottle.

## Here's what you need:

2 clear 2-liter plastic bottles, clean

duct tape

3 cups (¾ liter) of water

blue food coloring

# Making a Tornado in a Bottle

First, remove the labels from two 2-liter bottles. Then mix a few drops of food coloring into 3 cups (¾ liter) of water. Pour the colored water into one of the bottles.

Place the empty bottle
upside-down on top
of the first bottle.
Line up the openings.

Use duct tape to cover
the necks of the bottles.
Wrap the tape tightly
so the bottles
won't come apart.

Turn the bottles over
so the water is on top.
Watch as the water moves
slowly to the bottom.

Turn the bottles over again.

Quickly swirl the bottles
in a circle a few times.
Watch as a tornado appears!

# How Does It Work?

Real tornadoes happen
when hot air pushes up.
Wind whips around
a center point,
pulling cold air down.

wind
cold air
hot air

The tornado in the bottle works in a similar way. When the bottles are turned over, the air pushes up.

air

Swirling the bottles around
makes the water spin
around the center hole.
Like wind, the movement pulls
the water down.

# Glossary

**roar**—to make a loud, deep noise

**similar**—alike

**swirl**—to quickly move around in circles

**whip**—to quickly move with great force

# Read More

**Brunelle, Lynn.** *Big Science for Little People: 52 Activities to Help You and Your Child Discover the Wonders of Science.* Boulder, Colo.: Roost Books, 2016.

**Smibert, Angie.** *Mind-Blowing Physical Science Activities.* Curious Scientists. North Mankato, Minn.: Capstone Press, 2018.

**Sohn, Emily.** *Experiments in Earth Science and Weather with Toys and Everyday Stuff.* Fun Science. North Mankato, Minn.: Capstone Press, 2016.

# Internet Sites

Use FactHound to find Internet sites related to this book.

Visit *www.facthound.com*

Just type **9781543509441** and go.

# Critical Thinking Questions

1. Why is it important to wrap the tape tightly around the necks of the bottles?
2. What happens to the air inside when the bottles are turned over?
3. How does swirling the bottles around help to create a tornado inside of the top bottle?

# Index


air, 16, 18
duct tape, 10
food coloring, 6
labels, 6
pouring, 6
rain, 4
swirling, 14, 20
taping, 10
tornadoes, 4, 14, 16
water, 6, 12, 20
wind, 4, 16, 20